A COMPILATION OF FLOWERS

HOLLY MANNO

Edited by
JENNIFER L ROOP

Imprint: fraudess

Includes excerpts from previously or soon to be published work.

ISBN Ebook: 978-0-578-86472-3

ISBN Print: 978-1-7337869-9-7

ISBN Hardcover-Amazon: 9798778601086

ISBN Hardcover-Ingram: 979-8-8690-2908-9

EMPOWERMENT

Chapter One

A SON'S STRENGTH

It wasn't my own that rose from within.
My power came from him—a love born with him.
My value was unclear until he came through.
The months grew to jubilee—the day he was new.
This child of glory and hell bent to be.
He wasn't my charge dear—he came to save me.

I HAVE AN INCREDIBLE SON

Chapter Two

LEAVING THE NEST

The limb was thin and bending from her weight but the trunk, the branch where yesterday she'd perched herself so snuggly had become too constant. A voice spoke to her, taking control of her experience, leading her toward the web of sun speckled leaves and the new day where everything could change.

The moment she reached the thinnest section of branch, a snap so quiet and all together deafening, shot her down and incredibly forward, making her fly or die. It took a moment of free falling before her instincts joined her. With translucent wings, and her heart racing with hope, she launched into the next life.

Bubbles of excitement and hesitation pop, pop, popped at her chest. Was there ever any doubt she could fly?

A VIEW FROM THE TOP (NOVEL EXCERPT FROM LOVE TEST)

Climbing to the top can be quite scary, especially when you've been taught to fear the view.

JOY IS RIGHT

Grey does not commit.
    What choice can be made
    in a monochrome haze?

Black is always black.
    Darkness as a cloak,
    Abyss that should be smote.

Gold illuminates all.
    A compass to joy
    And joy is right…

TODAY I TOOK A WALK

Today I took a walk
Into the forest
Along gravel and mudded path
Where birds calls echoed
And oxygen ran amok.

The treetops roared
A hysterical whisper
Moody clouds covered the sun
Dirt hit my ankles
Crunch, glop, crunch, glob.

Wading through tall grass
Venturing off trail
Surrounded, mist and rotting wood
Intertwined with sweet blooms
Making the fear stop

Please, leave me here
My day comes
Fowl, rock and decaying plants
Soil and worms consume
Let me become earth.

Chapter Six

PATH

Sour belly
Sleepless night
Shaky palms
Today I set my path...

Fear rising
Fantastic dreams
Forge ahead
Today I walk my path...

Momentum sloth-ish
Merriment distant
Morose consideration
Today I pause my path...

Light dawning
Legacy awaits
Lead me home
Today I find my path...

Reckoning comes
Resistance squelched
Raised spirits
Today I become my path...

Chapter Seven

RESURRECTION

You broke me.
Pushed me down.
Took the last of my childish hope.
Why bother me still?
I've nothing left to swindle.
Nor give.
But wait,
Is it my resurrection?
Would you like that too?
I'm stronger now.
After mending myself.
Making energy for the worthy.
I won't open the door.
You'll never change.
It's true.
And yes,
My resurrection will be splendid…
Without you.

DAWNING

Chapter Eight

MORNING SKY

The sky is showing off again,
    Streaming her pinks and reds.
    Fizzled clouds float softly,
    Muting her light.
    But her glory can't be hidden,
    Like a secret or her shame.
    She'll shine again,
    Only brighter this time.

Chapter Nine

WE

A stream of geese fly by,

Forming a billowing ribbon in the sky.

Wings so closely cut,

They nearly touch.

There's no space between us.

Chapter Ten

A CAT CALLED WOMBAT

Barren black branches,
Crept in emerald,
Foreground of ancient limbs.
Layers of haze,
And gold and white,
Stairs to her crowning radiance.
A flock of chickadees,
Swoop and flutter,
Wings glisten–suspended.
Fervid beaks pummel moss,
Their morning feast,
Proves easy today.
I watch from my window,
Sated—not satisfied,
But I am home.

Chapter Eleven

MY WEAKNESS—INSPIRED BY HELIOS

My pilgrimage begins at dawn,

Unfurling golden ribbons.

You longed to drive my chariot home.

One day, a wish, my brother.

Your giddy irked to something foul.

It cracked your face a fiendish way.

A flaming whip—you scorched the earth.

Her smoking soul wastes at our hands.

Chapter Twelve

SLEEPING

Her glory shone—brilliant
In the early morning hours
A spectacle and private show.

Scarves of pink and vibrant gold
Against the geese trumpet
Broadcasting her arrival.

How many days have I slept
Missing her whisper-soft fingers
Against my cheek?

My darkness held me
Left her affections waiting—
Always, waiting.

Chapter Thirteen

DAWN TO FADE

Genesis unfurls from spindly reddened stems
Trained by the whims of the breeze
Unfolding a crown of magnificence

Microscopic advances
Earth to sky, sky to earth
Rising over night

Her shaken frame
A glory to behold
Determination emanates

Root and rock surge depths
Cares to detain
Tomorrow's breath

Opaque folds to diurnal
Begets night
Darkness reigns

Heavy eyes lose sight of the stars
Slumber of a life fought alone
Rest when the King ascends

(Previously published by "Tails from the Trails")

ISOLATION

Chapter Fourteen

VANISHED

Ever feel as though you could disappear
　　and it wouldn't make a ripple of difference?

Like the world is already preparing for your vacancy? Closing a little more each day until there's nothing to keep you.

ME

Taxes - Traitor
Debtor - Death
Certain - Choking
Workless - Worthless
Hunted - Haunted
Shirker - Shamed
Thief - Taker
Flounder - Failure
Useless - Useless
Bankrupt - Bankrupt
Bankrupt - Bankrupt

Chapter Sixteen

BOOKS AND SHOWS, PEN AND PAPER

That's wonderful, she thinks, and taps the heart icon. Smiling—she scrolls past images: distant friends, perfect families, vacations. She's happy for them and clear of envy, though part of her is sad. She knows he was right. Words she didn't want to hear rang ominously true.

> *I will be alone*
> *because I am separate,*
> *just as you made me.*
> *I watch from above*
> *without being present.*
> *Safe as an onlooker,*
> *untouched, unseen.*
> *When I suffocate from old damage*
> *and they hate me again,*
> *my love endures past tears.*
> *and books and shows,*
> *pen and paper*
> *hold my hope.*

MELANCHOLY FLASHBACK

Screaming silently
Yelling in my head
Flashing yesterday
Life I didn't dread
Tendrils tease
My red wine ways
Flirting breeze
I miss those days
Choices abound
Wish it could be
Higher ground
Land of the free

THE INVISIBLE LIFE

Yellow heat and taunting black spots

Unseen oxygen
Feeds pulse
Love once absorbed
Bound
Distance caresses
Family scrambled
Eggs against whisk
Tears
Lost, yet gloriously known

Yellow heat and taunting black spots

EMPTY

Filthy windows—day goes to night.
 Street lights.
 Monochrome haze.
 A rug of yarn—curved spine.
 Solitary catastrophe.
 Half-mast.
 Disconsolate heart—paper skin.
 She doesn't weep.
 Hollow eyes.
 Filthy windows—her day goes to night.

WEIGHTLESS

Drip, drop, plop.

Lavender oil.
    Black cherries and rose.
    Empty bottle and childproof lid.
    Flowing brightly.

Sleepy, sleep, slept.

FREAK

I DON'T KNOW HOW TO MAKE THIS RIGHT.
WISH I COULD JUST END OUR FIGHT.
IF I CAN'T MAKE IT THROUGH WITH YOU.
WHAT ELSE AM I GOING TO DO?

YOU ARE MY LIGHT—MY REASON WHY.
TO KNOW OUR STRIFE—MY FALLEN SKY.

I DO NOT WISH TO STAY THIS WAY.
PLEASE DON'T SAY TO GO AWAY.
YOU KNOW THAT I CAN'T SAY GOODBYE.
AND IF I DID, IT WOULD BE A LIE.

THIS IS THE PERSON—WHO I AM.
IF YOU CAN'T LOVE ME—NO ONE CAN.

INSCAPE

Gnarled beneath her pale skin
Coursing through her veins
Perils of history and lost files
Like her remains.

She tossed the key into the sea
No evidence or disdain
Her heart quit beating–chambers emptied
Vanishing her family's shame.

CRIMES

LESSONS

The lessons that I didn't learn
    Hanged by my missteps.
    I awake in the rainy night
    Haunted before the hillside's bulbs are lit
    The jagged edge of my inertia
    Prods me toward insanity
    I feel your shadow
    Your perversion exposed
    The stalker who lies in wait
    Yet *I* take your path

THEY DID IT

YOU
cannot
commit
suicide
when
you
have
already
been
murdered.

Chapter Twenty-Five

PUFFY WHITE

Summer will not come.
    I shiver under the atmosphere's tantrum.
    Puffy white clouds,
    like other puffy white things
    are fueled to dampen the sun,
    covering her goodness in shroud.

Chapter Twenty-Six

LIE

*Some
people
lie
with
the
kind
of
ease
that
others
save
only
for
breathing...*

THE NOOSE YOU DESERVE

The noose of your crimes
    Forever circles your collar
    Suspending your rot
    Dank, dry spoils
    Churn your guilty haunting
    Turning always
    Back to me
    The stain you
    Can never bleach
    Like the gritty film
    Between you

MOURNING

BALANCE

I ponder the irony as I sit in my backyard,
in the exact spot that took my balance
one fateful afternoon,
three years past.
This devilish piece of land
has thrice watched me twist,
crumbling under the shadow
of her impenetrable oak.
The God of a tree I worship,
a home that was to be my nest,
even the gnarled piece of earth,
thatched with clover and dandelion,
pocked beneath from roots and rodent,
I have loved them all
and today they see my end.
Today, I am buried.

THE FUNERAL

Your sweat is in the soil,
Voice echoes from the walls.
Drapes know you were the bass,
Watcher of me.
The raven has come,
To scratch me out.

My sweat is in the soil,
Voice echoes from the walls.
Drapes know I was the treble,
Watcher of thee.
I am the raven,
Go quiet—don't shout.

FAREWELL MY HOME

I thought you might lose your charms
Once stripped of your adornments
Without interesting baubles
Brightening your planks
And with nails as vacancy
Against the vast wood walls.
But you did not…
The sheen of heaven floats around
Dances against your angles
Highlighting the best bones
And your timeless appeal.
Your welcome, astounds…
Naked before me—unmasked—unmade
You remain extraordinary
Twinkles and gashes collide
Evidence of your travels.
An ageless vintage.
The love you have witnessed
And even the tears

Holds you—aloof—above
In your deserved place.
Oh, how I'll miss you.
Farewell my home…

Chapter Thirty-One

AN ACCIDENT

They called it an accident
As your blood poured onto the streets
And your lungs filled wrongly.

The steel couldn't hold you
My love didn't stop it
GOD left my prayers in the ocean.

Horror confines me
With impossible permanence
Steps cannot heal.

We called it an accident
As your blood filled my womb
And my lungs shrunk themselves.
For you

Chapter Thirty-Two

TWO SISTERS

We took the awkward path,
Where forest meets sea.
His sky grew dim.
Gust at our elbows.
Shoved relentlessly ahead.
Facing the murky sea.
Merciless waves cracked eternal.
Jutted with rocks and sorrow.
Then God, in his unapologetic light,
Graced us with his halo.
Green leaves glistened.
Air became sweet.
A fine mist to swallow.
Facade to Joy.
Bring him back,
Or take me too.

Chapter Thirty-Three

TO KRISTIN FROM THE VAIN GIRLS

I'm sorry dear friend, we lost our way.
    We won't get to waste another Sunday.

T's Bloody Mary's and a belly full of grease
    The best giggle session—our favorite release.

Story from the night before
    True as much as we adore.

Your baby doll swirled too high.
    I liked it when we touched the sky.

Chiffon and lace, the hairbands too
    I can't believe that we are through.

.   .   .

To never hear you laugh and say,
    "Now, aren't you glad I made you stay?"

No one knows what happens now,
    You didn't get to take a bow.

You were the light that shone for us,
    I won't believe you'll turn to dust.

Know that you will always remain
    Shining star–we'll meet again.

OH LOVE, YOUR DAGGER IS SO SWEET...

Chapter Thirty-Four

EYES LOCK

People write about it, sing about it, talk about it yet, the mystery and power remain. What is it that happens when your eyes lock, not every time but those crucial instances, when your eyes meet another's and the undercurrent of knowledge holds you, confirming all you cannot see, touch, or feel? Like air, the power is there yet you are unable to grasp it. What does this moment mean and how that will affect your life? For you know it will.

-Excerpt from ANCHOR of GOLD, a novel.

NEW SUNRISE

WAKING
UP
NEXT
TO
YOU
FEELS
LIKE
THE
SUN
IS
RISING
IN
MY
CHEST

Chapter Thirty-Six

ANCHOR OF GOLD (NOVEL EXCERPT)

"Wait," he said, the stranger I didn't know.
I kept walking, embarrassed by my tears.
He saw me, all of me, yet he didn't leave.
Gentle fingers soothed, gave hope.
His left hand weighted by an anchor of gold.

Wary, trying not, but needing him;
I rode the wheel,
Present in every way,
It was all and it was unstoppable.
We exist in the confine of moment.
Held entranced by our eyes,
though his left hand wore an anchor of gold.

Did he feel the surge,
my feminine need to be owned by him?
Did he care?
An illusion some say,

but I stood taller by his side,
and the dust blew away from my soul.
My lips, my lungs, my heart drew in,
greedy to soak up every particle he could spare,
crumbs that were left by his anchor of gold.

Still, I may have the best of it.
Once, pineapples and spies.
I will remember him softly.
Cheese, make a wish, say goodbye.
I hope you are blessed by your anchor of gold.

TEMPTATION ROSE

His calls were insistent
    A silent assault
    Fingers along spine
    Felt but not seen
    Need and want commingled.

I lingered with bated breath
    Craving to know
    What's not mine to learn
    To touch that splintered soul
    Possess him—all ways.

GOLDEN CHAIN WITH A BROKEN LINK

Lay in the snow—
    Be with me.
    Forget everything
    We can't see.

Trip over impossible—
    Rays in my eyes.
    We're not responsible
    Don't question our lies.

Marking our territory—
    Permanent ink.
    Emblazon our glory,
    Golden chain with a broken link.

Chapter Thirty-Nine

THE SWEETEST KISS

The sweetest kiss I ever knew,
The sweetest kiss belonged to you.
You loaned it once—you loaned it twice.
It made me think that you were right.
The spell wore off and then I knew,
The sweetest kiss, it was not true.
You broke me down with each caress.
You lied to me and made a mess.
Although I know you weren't mine,
I still daydream for your smooth lines.
You breezed on in and out my life,
And now each day is like a knife.
The sweetest kiss I ever knew,
The sweetest kiss belonged to WHO?

Chapter Forty

ONLY DREAMING

That hopeful soft spot
I thought was real
may have been imagined.

WAIT FOR IT

I live for the slow,
    quiet mornings in your eyes.

The proprietary curve of
    your fingers against my ribs.

Our shared breath
    confining us in divinity.

If only as we sleep.

DEAD IGNITION

And fit they did
A key and an ignition
Driving through all the dark places
Those long-abandoned trails
Until the black faded to grey, then orange.
As heaven turned to Dawn
Their bond—sealed
Cells took up residence.
A forgotten womb remembered
The gasp of Joy
Halo against shadows, against evil
Hiding places inside the clouds
But his light was fading ink,
Silence louder than her beatless heart
Vacancy of the damned—no car explodes.

Chapter Forty-Three

THE LEADERSHIP OF ME

I gave you what you didn't know you wanted
    The license to make my choices

I surrendered my will to your whims
    And floated no ideas by you

I did it because I couldn't move anymore
    Life pulled me in every direction

Surrender wasn't as hard as I'd expected
    You wore my burden like a King

Holding me though you were weary
    But eventually, you loathed me

· · ·

My demands whispered to your conscience
  I believed you could handle everything

Your shoulders seemed so sturdy
  But your eyes filled with contempt

And your body cooled against mine
  I took more than my share

And squandered my listless time
  Your fancy was lost to conquest

A victory you never sought
  The leadership of me.

Chapter Forty-Four

PEOPLE GET LOST

Because people get lost sometimes. They get lost in their lives and forget the slow twist of the leaf as it makes its descent from the branch to the soft grass beneath its belly.

They forget how a gentle breeze is a gift from the past, transporting them to another place in time. A day when the sun warmed their skin.

Chapter Forty-Five

FIREWORKS

There were no fireworks.
No music rang out.
To say it was dramatic is true,
but not in the way you'd think.
I should have been awed speechless.
He is all that.
I was enthralled—but in ease.
The air changed.
It became lighter somehow.
He stood and I thought of the stars.

Chapter Forty-Six

NAKED

"I hoped you'd see me naked from the first time I set eyes on you."

He dove for me then, his hands were in my hair and his mouth covered mine. The taste of *finally* commingled with the mint of his tongue, and it was on. He ripped my blouse open. I responded by tearing his drawers to his ankles. Our first time was on the fifth stair. We couldn't make it to the bedroom. Our bond was sealed as his hands held my face and together—we let go.

Chapter Forty-Seven

ABOUT LOVE

About love…

I don't think it goes away. Once you've given someone that much, opened yourself to their soul, you will always feel the glint of a flame at your heart and the threat of tears tickling your eyes.

PRIMROSE

The forest
You
My heart
In two
First
And
Always
My breath
You drew
Tears unchecked
Your fancy cooled
I wander
Terra
Empty
Blue
For no one else will ever do.

FAITH?

DO YOU BELIEVE IN GOD?

Yes.

Sometimes.

Most Times.

Not All The Time.

Not Today.

When I Pray.

I Don't Know.

Yes.

TIES

Ties may bind
and some do bite.
The scars of history
stop our flight.
It's not your mind
that isn't right.
The ropes that hold
are made of light.

STARGAZING

Your whisper soothed my lonesome ears,
A chant of dreams and light.

The moon and son grow oh so near.
I grasp with all my might.

Our glitter burst and settled, dear.
Some things we cannot fight.

But when you cracked—
Without a tear, I gave him all my light.

WELCOME TO THE KING

A shock of dizzy ailment.
Swelling in her womb.
Domain of a king.
Adoration guides.
The destiny of a vessel.
She kneels then bows.
A kick through stretched skin.
The searing agony comes.
Water and blood and soul pour out.
Eternal slave—she's become.

REAL PINCE

Wheat beige hair
    and clear green eyes

You are of majesty
    no way to disguise.

That brilliant mind
    and those strong ways

You're the brightest star
    keep me–amazed.

I know you'll be the kindest soul
    the one who makes it right

And even when I'm very old
    I'll love you with all my might.

Chapter Fifty-Four

PRINCESS ETHEREAL

Princess ethereal,
    with pebbly toes,
    those piercing blue eyes,
    and buttony nose.

Most gorgeous of mind,
    with the kindest heart,
    you held me captive,
    from the start.

A ray from heaven,
    your aura—indeed,
    without you, darling,
    there's nothing to see.

Chapter Fifty-Five

GREAT WHITE OAK TREE

Do you feel my fingers against your belly,
    pressing tears into your bark?
    This way I leave you,
    wishing we never had to part.
    My heart lingers there,
    pray you live one-thousand years.
    Will you grow to the clouds
    and past them too?
    Can you sprout straight to GOD
    surrounded by blue?
    Might you sing with your leaves,
    and dare with your strength?
    Drop your seeds all around,
    your best endures-*F A I T H*.

Chapter Fifty-Six

AFTERLIFE

Tonight, I am the fortune teller
Future known by me
Around the world
An airplane crashes into the sea
The darkest night
Black waters, ice
Mothers, children
Rescuers-fight
Waves to the tunnel
That glows in the deep
A glance that direction
Puts each soul at ease
Move forward-to glory
Make everything new
You're almost home now
So happy it's true.

ACKNOWLEDGMENTS

This compilation wasn't ready to be published until I came across a piece written by my son, back in 2010. His poem, I Love You, Mama, reminded me that even in the darkest of situations, love is evergreen. For now, his words will stay between us, a memory and the sentiment of a young man who was just beginning his journey into adulthood.

It is an early January morning as I write. I sit facing east (I have a thing about this). Through the grainy 80-year-old glass window, I watch the rapid mood swings of Portland, Oregon's weather unfold. It's show-time again. A grey, tornado shaped cloud dances above Mt. Hood, and a stream of melancholy comforters ripple along the pines to hover above the Willamette River. The coffee pot beeps, announcing the burner has shut off. My adored dog is snug in a burgundy wool blanket and the cat is finally asleep after another night of spasticity (Cats are tidy roommates, but they party every night). My family is safe, but I—like many of you—am reeling.

2020 was a remarkable and devastating year for the globe. With all that happened, at times I was depressed, anxious, and even angry. As it relates to writing, I had plans and hopes for the year that vanished along with my good credit. The isolation, political climate and fallout of events affected me on many levels.

Something that helped me cope and continue writing, was poetry. The following micro-collection of poems and musings explore many different subjects. Some of the pieces are depressing or seething while others are romantic and hopeful. Like the weather, my moods shift and these tiny stories paint the pictures of my heart.

Thank you for reading and reviewing my books.

Holly

P.S. A special thanks to the Willamette Writers for their support and creating a community around words. There were a few specific including Rebecca, John & Katie who helped this project along.

ALSO BY HOLLY MANNO

LOVE TEST, Book I in the series

ALSO BY HOLLY MANNO

Times Two, Book II in the LOVE TEST series